SPECIAL REPORTS

THE WORLD'S WILDFIRES

BY REBECCA ROWELL

CONTENT CONSULTANT
Crystal Raymond, PhD
Climate Adaptation Specialist
Climate Impacts Group
University of Washington

Essential Library
An Imprint of Abdo Publishing | abdobooks.com

abdobooks.com

Published by Abdo Publishing, a division of ABDO, PO Box 398166, Minneapolis, Minnesota 55439.

Printed in the United States of America, North Mankato, Minnesota.
102020
012021

Cover Photo: Francisco Seco/AP Images
Interior Photos: Megan Juresa/Abaca/Sipa USA/AP Images, 4–5; Twitter@NSWRFS/AP Images, 7; Kiran Ridley/Polaris/Newscom, 9; Rick Rycroft/AP Images, 14, 88; Joe Armao/The Age/Fairfax Media/Getty Images, 16–17; Erich Schlegel/AP Images, 18–19; Viesinsh/Alamy, 21; Shutterstock Images, 24; Morphius Film/Shutterstock Images, 26; Jann Huizenga/iStockphoto, 28; Christian Roberts-Olsen/Shutterstock Images, 30–31; Geoff Spencer/AP Images, 35; Ted S. Warren/AP Images, 37; Josh Edelson/AP Images, 38–39; Jae C. Hong/AP Images, 41; John R. Foster/Science Source, 44; Al Grillo/AP Images, 48–49; Marcio Jose Sanchez/AP Images, 54, 82–83; Karl Anderson/The Courier/AP Images, 60; Zhuravlev Andrey/Shutterstock Images, 63; Genaro Molina/Los Angeles Times/AP Images, 64–65; Noah Berger/AP Images, 66–67; Eric Risberg/AP Images, 71; Kristina Barker/Rapid City Journal/AP Images, 74–75; Francisco Seco/AP Images, 77; Scott G Winterton/Deseret News/AP Images, 79; Jay Janner/Austin American-Statesman/AP Images, 84–85; Mike Meadows/AP Images, 94; Mike Eliason/Santa Barbara County Fire Department/AP Images, 96–97

Editor: Charly Haley
Series Designer: Maggie Villaume

Library of Congress Control Number: 2020940449

Publisher's Cataloging-in-Publication Data

Names: Rowell, Rebecca, author.
Title: The world's wildfires / by Rebecca Rowell
Description: Minneapolis, Minnesota : Abdo Publishing, 2021 | Series: Special reports | Includes online resources and index
Identifiers: ISBN 9781532194184 (lib. bdg.) | ISBN 9781098213541 (ebook)
Subjects: LCSH: Wildfires--Climatic factors--Juvenile literature. | Climatic changes--Juvenile literature. | Forest biodiversity--Effect of fires on--Juvenile literature. | Post-fire forest management--Juvenile literature. | Reforestation--Climatic factors--Juvenile literature.
Classification: DDC 363.379--dc23

CONTENTS

CHAPTER ONE

AUSTRALIA BURNING

On December 31, 2019, as the world was celebrating New Year's Eve, thousands of people on Australia's southeastern coast went to the beach. It was summer, and beaches are a favorite spot for the region's many residents and tourists. The sky was red and smoky, but celebratory fireworks were not the cause. The thousands of people were not at the beaches for fun or to celebrate. Rather, they were seeking refuge from what seemed like the end of the world. Australia was burning. Wildfires were scorching the land, destroying buildings, and killing animals and people.

The large amounts of smoke from wildfires, such as the smoke seen in Australia on December 31, 2019, can turn the sky red because of how sunlight shines through the smoke.

Approximately 4,000 people fled from Mallacoota, a town in eastern Victoria, one of Australia's six states. In the neighboring state of New South Wales (NSW), hundreds of families in the town of Batemans Bay ran from the fires as well. Zoe Simmons was among them. She told the news network CNN, "It was like we were in hell. We were all covered in ash."[1]

EARLY FIRE SEASON

Such fires were not new in Australia. In fact, they are such regular occurrences that the country has a fire season. It happens from December to February, during Australia's summer, and usually peaks in late January or early February. In 2019, however, the fire season began approximately three months early. In addition, the fires were considerably worse than usual. NSW was hit especially hard by the wildfires. More than 13 million acres (5 million ha) of the region's land burned, taking with it 2,500 houses.[2] NSW is home to Sydney, Australia's most populous city.

Australians refer to their wildfires as *bushfires*. The 2019–20 bushfire season began on October 26, 2019, with a lightning strike at Gospers Mountain, NSW. The resulting blaze would become Australia's largest-ever forest fire to begin with a single starting point, ravaging one million acres (444,000 ha).[3] That same day, a thunderstorm started a fire in Port Macquarie, NSW. Two days later, on October 28, the 2019–20 fire season claimed its first life as a fire near Cattai, NSW, scorched 29,653 acres (12,000 ha) of land.[4] Firefighters worked to contain the blazes. Air tankers dropped fire retardant. Helicopters dropped water. On November 20, a fire started in Yorke Peninsula, South

Australia's firefighters, many of whom were volunteers, worked for up to 18 hours at a time to contain the bushfires in 2019 and 2020.

Australia. Authorities think an electrical transformer started the blaze, which destroyed 12,355 acres (5,000 ha) and 11 houses.[5]

Fires continued in December. On December 5, 42 firefighters from the United States and Canada arrived to help battle the fires. On December 15, a fire burning near the NSW towns of Mount Wilson and Mount Irvine grew out of control, destroying 864,868 acres (350,000 ha).[6] Then, on December 19, a fire truck was engulfed. Firefighters made an emergency exit out of the truck. Three firefighters were hospitalized for burn treatment. More firefighters from the United States and Canada joined the fight against Australia's blazes.

AUSTRALIA'S BUSHFIRE SEASON

Bushfires can occur in Australia throughout the year, and their likelihood varies by region and season. According to Australia's Bureau of Meteorology, "Bushfire activity varies across Australia with the changes in the seasonal weather patterns. Wind, temperature, humidity, and rainfall are weather elements that affect the behaviors of bushfires."[7] Summer is the most dangerous season for fires in much of Australia, including in NSW and Victoria. Being in the Southern Hemisphere, Australia's seasons are opposite those of the United States. That is, summer in Australia occurs when the United States is experiencing winter. Bushfires raged in the Australian summer from late 2019 to early 2020.

Less than two weeks later, on December 26, a lightning strike started yet another fire. The blaze in Sterling

The 2019–20 bushfires destroyed many people's homes and farms.

Ranges, Western Australia, burned 98,842 (40,000 ha) of park land. A few days later, on December 30, three more fires began in East Gippsland, Victoria, covering 321,236 acres (130,000 ha).[8] Australian authorities urged residents and visitors to evacuate. On December 31, as 2019 came to an end, three fires in NSW that had burned more than 635,061 acres (257,000 ha) united to form one massive blaze.[9]

RESIDENTS IN DANGER

Also on December 30, Australian authorities encouraged approximately 100,000 people living in suburbs around the city of Melbourne to evacuate. The state of Victoria's official alert system sent an emergency warning to residents of Noorinbee, which is 230 miles (600 km) east of Melbourne. The warning said, "You are in danger and need to act immediately to survive."[10]

In January 2020, the wildfires numbered in the dozens and showed no signs of slowing down, let alone stopping. Each of Australia's six states had experienced bushfires, with NSW getting the worst of the damage. More firefighters from the United States and Canada went to Australia to help. Neighboring New Zealand sent troops and equipment, adding to

AUSTRALIA'S FIRES AFFECT NEW ZEALAND

Although New Zealand sits more than 1,000 miles (1,600 km) off the coast of Australia, the country still suffered negative effects from Australia's 2019–20 fires. The skies filled with orange smoke. Air pollution increased, worsening the air quality. This was especially dangerous for people with respiratory conditions such as asthma. The smoke also caused events for tourists to be canceled.

Australia's bushfires affected New Zealand's glaciers too. The glaciers turned pink as dust and ash landed on the mountains of ice and rock. Having a darker color makes glaciers melt faster. Melting glaciers is a problem for multiple reasons. First, it causes sea levels to rise, which can result in flooding and habitat destruction. Second, ice reflects sunlight. Less ice means less sunlight is reflected and more of that sunlight is absorbed by Earth, warming the planet. Finally, some animals live in icy places and need the glaciers to survive. The good news is that the pink in New Zealand's glaciers was expected to be temporary, lasting only one season.

the 157 firefighters from New Zealand already fighting the flames.[11]

Major cities such as Melbourne, Sydney, and Canberra, Australia's capital, did not burn. But they were not immune to the effects of the fires. Dense smoke blanketed some cities, making breathing difficult for people. As a result, Melbourne closed beaches and pools, and officials canceled some sporting events. Outdoor workers, such as those doing construction, had to stop working. The number of emergency calls about people having breathing problems increased dramatically.

Melbourne's poor air quality prompted the Australian Medical Association (AMA) to advise people to be cautious. Specifically, the organization highlighted the heightened risk to those with heart or lung issues and those who are

AUSTRALIAN OPEN

Each January, Melbourne hosts the Australian Open, the first of professional tennis's four big tournaments. In 2020, tennis players from around the world faced the city's polluted air. Some struggled to play their matches. At least one player fell to her knees in a coughing fit. The fires forced tournament organizers to deal with air-quality issues, including developing an air-quality policy. Meteorological and air-quality experts worked on-site to assess air quality during the tournament. Craig Tiley, the tournament's director, said, "This is a new experience for all of us in how we manage air quality, so we have to listen to the experts."[12]

sensitive to smoke. Many people bought respirators—masks that go over the mouth and nose—that are typically worn by housepainters and other workers to protect them from fumes. The AMA also said that people planning to visit Australia should bring masks.

CONTAINING THE FIRES

By January 31, fires had scorched more than 27 million acres (11 million ha) of Australia's landscape. More than 30 people had died, including four firefighters.[13] Weather conditions had shifted, offering cooler temperatures and even some rain. But more than 50 fires continued to burn in NSW and Victoria.

A positive development finally came on February 13 when firefighters contained Australia's wildfires. It was the first time the fires had been contained since September 2019. Rob Rogers, the deputy commissioner of the NSW Rural Fire Service, spoke about the importance of the containment, calling it "great news." He said, "[Now] we can really focus on helping people rebuild."[14]

MORE TO THE STORY

AUSTRALIA'S GUM TREES

Australia is home to forests of eucalyptus trees, which Australians call gum trees. The trees are the sole food source for the beloved koala. These marsupials also rely on the trees for shelter and safety. Eucalyptus forests are critical for koalas to survive. Gum trees also fuel wildfires. Eucalyptus leaves blanket the ground when they fall, and eucalyptus bark comes off the tree in long strips. Both the leaves and bark are flammable. Strips of bark hanging down from trees can draw flames into the treetops in what is called a crown fire. Eucalyptus trees have an oil that gives them their distinctive fragrance. That oil is also flammable.

David Bowman, a forest ecologist at Australia's University of Tasmania, spoke with a California public radio station about Australia's wildfires after the 2013 fire season, which destroyed hundreds of homes and affected eucalyptus trees. Bowman said, "Looking at the eucalyptus forest outside my window in Tasmania, I see a gigantic fire hazard. On a really hot day, those things are going to burn like torches and shower our suburbs with sparks."[15] However, despite this damage, eucalyptus forests need some wildfires. Fires allow trees to resprout and new habitat to grow.

Even after the fires were mostly contained in early 2020, firefighters had to keep working to keep the fires under control and prevent new fires.

UNDERSTANDING WILDFIRES

Australia's 2019–20 bushfire season was one of the worst the island nation had experienced to date. As Australia burned, many people—Australians and others around the world—speculated about the role of climate change in the disaster. Countless people were certain that the changing climate had contributed to the severity of the fires.

Australia's experience can serve as an example for other nations. Destructive wildfires like those Australia suffered during the 2019–20 bushfire season are not confined to Australia. For example, in the United States, California regularly faces wildfires. Blazes there and in other parts of the western United States also highlight the effects of climate change. They point to another issue, too: encroachment. This refers to building houses and other structures in or near areas known to have wildfires, putting people in harm's way. Meanwhile, fires in other regions of the world bring attention to the effects of intentional burning carried out to clear forests for other uses.

"I AM STANDING HERE A TRAVELER FROM A NEW REALITY, A BURNING AUSTRALIA. WHAT WAS FEARED AND WHAT WAS WARNED IS NO LONGER IN OUR FUTURE, A TOPIC FOR DEBATE—IT IS HERE. WE HAVE SEEN THE UNFOLDING WINGS OF CLIMATE CHANGE."[16]

—LYNETTE WALLWORTH, AUSTRALIAN FILMMAKER, JANUARY 2020

Wildfires have a variety of causes and effects. Understanding the many aspects of wildfires—including how they start, how to fight them, and how to prepare for them—can help mitigate their destructive results.

FROM THE HEADLINES

THE ANIMALS

As forests and other landscapes burn, the animals living there are forced to flee. Many die. Estimates for the loss of animal life in the 2019–20 bushfire season vary. According to Mihir Zaveri and Emily S. Rueb of the *New York Times*, "Experts in biodiversity have expressed alarm at the span of scorched Earth in a megadiverse country that harbors between 600,000 to 700,000 species, many [of] which are not found anywhere else in the world."[17]

Christopher Dickman, an ecology professor at the University of Sydney, estimated that 480 million animals died in NSW alone during the 2019 fires. That was before the fires were put out. He revised the number in January 2020 to more than 800 million. In an interview with National Public Radio, Dickman said, "It's events like this that may well hasten the extinction process for a range of other species. So, it's a very sad time."[18]

But these numbers are estimates, and researchers have no way of knowing the actual loss of life. Corey Bradshaw, a professor of global ecology at Australia's Flinders University, said, "The media and the public in general are hungry for numbers, and

Emergency animal-care units helped koalas and other animals during the Australia bushfires in 2020.

they get into a fuss, but the reality is no one actually knows." He added, "We are constantly surprised how recovery happens quickly after a fire and how many animals survive."[19]

WILDFIRE BASICS

Having a basic understanding of wildfires is critical to having meaningful discussions about them. Understanding wildfires includes knowing what they are, what they are called, and what leads to the different names. It also includes understanding where these fires occur and how they behave. Additionally, it is important to recognize that while wildfires damage property and habitats, they are also necessary to keep habitats healthy.

DEFINING AND NAMING WILDFIRES

A wildfire is an uncontrolled fire in wildland vegetation. Wildfires occur in different types of vegetation,

Wildfires do not only burn in forests. They also affect grasslands and other types of vegetation.

including trees, shrubs, and grasses. Wildfires burn in forests, grasslands, and savannas.

Wildfires are sometimes called by other names, such as *brush fire* or *forest fire*. The term used reflects the vegetation being burned and where the fire is burning. Brush fires occur in vegetation shorter than six feet (1.8 m). Forest fires burn in growth taller than six feet (1.8 m).

Wildfires can be categorized as ground, surface, or crown. Ground fires burn on or below the forest floor, including down into the soil. Underground, they can feed on the roots of plants. Usually, these fires smolder and do not have flames. This type of wildfire can smolder for a long time. With the right conditions, a ground fire can become a surface fire or a crown fire.

Surface fires burn along the forest floor. They involve many types of vegetation. Some, such as dead leaves or dry grass, is very close to the ground. But surface fires also burn dead wood and live plants, such as shrubs. Surface fires are generally slow-moving, but in open, grassy areas they can move very fast. They can be highly destructive to trees, damaging or killing them.

Crown fires occur in the higher parts of vegetation, such as the leaves and canopies of trees and shrubs. These fires move quickly. They jump from treetop to treetop with the help of wind. Crown fires are the most destructive type of wildfire.

While wildfires are destructive to plants and animals in some ways, they are also a necessary and important part of plant growth. For example, a wildfire blackened one-third of Yellowstone National Park in 1988. Some news

While surface fires burn on the ground, they can become crown fires when they spread to the higher parts cf trees and other plants.

sources said the park was destroyed. But that was not the case. Native grasses and wildflowers quickly sprouted. Lodgepole pine seedlings grew in the areas where the forests had burned. In these ways, much of Yellowstone's natural landscape was renewed.

"PLANTS HAVE EVOLVED DIFFERENT STRATEGIES TO COPE WITH FIRE. ONE STRATEGY IS TO SURVIVE FIRE AS A SEED, NOT AS AN INDIVIDUAL PLANT."[1]

–ÇAĞATAY TAVŞANOĞLU, FIRE ECOLOGIST AT HACETTEPE UNIVERSITY IN TURKEY

THE INGREDIENTS OF FIRE

Fire requires three ingredients: heat, fuel, and oxygen. Without enough of these three ingredients, fire is not possible. A heat source is needed to ignite, or start, a fire. Then the fire feeds on fuel and is sustained by oxygen.

Fuel for a fire is anything that can burn. Moisture is an important factor in fuel. The less moisture something has, the better it will fuel a fire. This is why dry, dead leaves burn quicker than living leaves, which have moisture inside. The size, shape, quantity, and arrangement of fuel across a landscape affects how a fire burns and spreads.

Oxygen is also necessary for fire. Earth's atmosphere is approximately 21 percent oxygen. Fire needs at least

16 percent oxygen to burn, so normal air is excellent for fire, including wildfires.[2]

In addition to starting fires, heat keeps fires going in multiple ways. First, heat dries moisture in nearby fuel and warms the fuel. Second, heat warms the surrounding air. These two things help fire travel more easily. Heat readies the path for fire to move.

OXIDATION

Fire is more than a combination of the ingredients heat, fuel, and oxygen. Fire is a chemical reaction called combustion. As a wildfire burns the fuels in its path, including brush, trees, and houses, it reacts with oxygen in the surrounding air. Wildfires use up oxygen in a process called oxidation, and that oxidation causes the embers, heat, and smoke that are characteristic of a fire.

WILDFIRE CAUSES

Wildfires have a variety of causes. Some occur naturally, sparked by a lightning strike or ignited by the heat of the sun. Most wildfires are started by people. According to the National Interagency Fire Center, 87 percent of wildfires in the United States in 2019 were caused by humans.[3] Sometimes people set fires intentionally. But more often, wildfires are the result of careless actions.

Arson and prescribed burning are intentional causes. Arson is setting a fire on purpose to cause damage, and it is a crime. An example would be setting a building on fire to get insurance money. Prescribed burning, also called controlled burning, is when fires are set to clear land for agriculture or industry. If something goes wrong, these fires can turn into wildfires. There are also unintentional human causes of wildfires, such as campfires, fireworks, and lit cigarettes. For instance, campers might think they have put out a fire when it is still smoldering. If it is not fully extinguished, it may grow into a large blaze.

FIRE BEHAVIOR

Three factors influence wildfire behavior, or how wildfires move and change. These factors are weather, topography,

Unattended campfires can accidentally grow into wildfires.

and fuel. Weather consists of humidity, precipitation, temperature, and wind. High temperatures and winds can fuel wildfires, helping them grow in size and strength. Humidity and precipitation have the opposite effect. They can hinder wildfires by putting moisture in the air and on fuels. Without humidity and precipitation, fuels dry out, which makes them more flammable. This is one reason droughts cause concern. Areas suffering from drought become prone to wildfires because the vegetation dries out.

Topography can also help or hinder a fire's movement. Topography is a landscape's features, such as hills and lakes. The shape of the land affects wildfire movement. For example, wildfires typically move faster uphill than downhill. As heat from the flames rises, fuel uphill dries out more. The newly dried fuel catches fire more quickly than fuel downhill of the fire. Location affects fire movement, too. Fires are more likely to burn on the southern and western areas of hills and mountains. Because southern and western areas get more sun, they are usually drier than northern and eastern areas.

Wildfires can occur on mountains, and they move faster uphill than downhill.

Fuel characteristics that play a role in fire behavior are arrangement, moisture, and weight. Arrangement refers to how fuels are situated. An even, continuous layer of fuel, such as dried leaves and branches, helps wildfires spread and grow. Fuels that are lighter and drier catch fire more easily and feed fires more readily than fuels that are heavier and wetter. For example, it is very difficult to light a campfire with wet wood, large pieces of wood, or wood that does not touch other pieces of fuel.

STUDYING WILDFIRES

Researchers around the world study wildfires to learn how they behave and how they affect the environment and people. Researchers explore wildfires past, present, and future. The United States alone has several wildfire research organizations and projects.

The US Geological Survey (USGS) has a project that focuses on Southern California, an area that regularly experiences wildfires. The project is the Southern California Risk Scenario Project, and its researchers are studying patterns in wildfires that have reached urban areas. These scientists hope to discover why some communities burn while others do not. They study a variety of information, including housing patterns, wind patterns, vegetation, and the locations of power lines, to find a reason for this important difference.

Another federal agency, the US Forest Service, also researches wildfires. The Forest Service, alongside

NATURAL FUELS

The natural fuels that feed forest fires are classified as aerial, surface, and ground. Aerial fuels are at least 39 inches (99 cm) above the ground. Tree bark, branches, and leaves still attached to trees and bushes are some examples of aerial fuels. Surface fuels are the next level of natural fuels. These fuels are on the forest floor and include fallen branches, cones, leaves, and needles. Live bushes and other vegetation, as well as logs and tree stumps, are also surface fuels. Ground fuels are the materials that are in the ground. These items, which include plant roots and rotting materials such as branches, leaves, and needles, are fuels located below the surface.

FIRE DANGER
VERY HIGH
TODAY!
PREVENT FOREST FIRES
SMOKEY
SMOKEY

the National Park Service and the Bureau of Land Management, maintains the country's forests and grasslands. Achieving that mission includes researching how fires behave and how to best manage or prevent them.

Some scientists doing work related to wildfires are studying weather and climate conditions. They want to determine the likelihood of wildfires. For example, in December 2012, National Aeronautics and Space Administration (NASA) researchers used computer programs to make a prediction about wildfires in the United Sates based on data from satellites. Their findings suggested that conditions would be drier and wildfires would get worse over the next 30 to 50 years.[4] Specifically, wildfire seasons would last longer and have more intense or larger fires.

Continued research on wildfires will add to the understanding of these events. Governments, firefighters, and others can use this knowledge to help the environment and wildlife and to protect people.

The US Forest Service uses signs to warn campers at national parks about the possibility of starting a wildfire.

A HISTORY OF WILDFIRES

Wildfires are not new occurrences. For thousands of years, habitats have adapted to fires. Wildfires allow new plant growth and bring nutrients back to the soil. However, they can also damage cities and other aspects of human life. These fires occur around the world, including in the United States. A look at some of the numerous wildfires that have happened in the last 150 years gives a glimpse into the impact they can have on human life.

1870s TO MID-1900s

On October 8, 1871, the worst forest fires recorded in North America happened in Wisconsin and Michigan. The fires burned on both sides of Green Bay, the part

Wildfires have always been a part of nature.

WHAT IS AN ACRE?

The sizes of wildfires are often measured in acres or hectares. Historically, an acre was the area of land a farmer could plow in one day. At the time, an acre was long and skinny, only 22 yards wide and 220 yards long. Today, an acre is any area that measures 4,840 square yards (4,425 sq m). One acre is approximately the size of a soccer field. A hectare, in the metric system, is equivalent to approximately 2.47 acres.

of Lake Michigan that cuts into Wisconsin. As they burned, the fires, collectively called the Peshtigo Fire, destroyed villages and farms.

Experts think the Peshtigo Fire started in Peshtigo, Wisconsin. The blaze burned in northern Wisconsin and in Michigan's Upper Peninsula. The fire's destruction was massive, scorching 1.2 million acres (486,000 ha) of land and 17 towns. The estimated damage was $169 million.[1] That amount in 2020 would be equivalent to more than $3.5 billion. Greater than the loss of items was the loss of human lives. As many as 2,500 people died, more than in any other fire in US history.[2] Debra Anderson, an archivist at the University of Wisconsin–Green Bay Area Research Center, discussed the fire with a reporter from the *Green Bay Press-Gazette*. Anderson said, "What most researchers find so fascinating is the effect [the Peshtigo Fire] had on people's lives. It was so horrific. Some people thought it was the end of the world."[3]

Almost 40 years after the Peshtigo Fire, the Big Burn occurred between August 20 and 21, 1910. This wildfire in Idaho, Montana, and Washington burned three million acres (1.2 million ha) of forest. The Big Burn, which covered an area the size of Connecticut, was more than twice as large as the Peshtigo Fire. Seventy-eight firefighters and seven residents died.[4] The Big Burn is considered the largest wildfire in US history.

In 1918, the small town of Cloquet, Minnesota, experienced a horrific wildfire. In October, a train traveling through the town sent sparks flying near the tracks. The hot sparks ignited dry brush along the tracks. A wildfire grew rapidly, eventually burning more than 250,000 acres (101,000 ha). It consumed 38 towns.[5] Hundreds of people died. An additional 52,000 people were left hurt or homeless.[6]

The following year, five million acres (2 million ha) of land in western Canada burned in the Great Fire of 1919. The blaze began north of the city of Edmonton and spread quickly, fueled by wood that had been cut for timber. The fire burned hundreds of homes and killed 11 people.[7]

In 1939, Victoria, Australia, had the worst fires in its history to that point. The Black Friday bushfires burned almost five million acres (2 million ha), destroying entire towns in its path.[8] At least 71 people died.[9]

LATE 1900s

A few decades later, the Daxing'anling Wildfire caused great destruction in northeastern China. The blaze started on May 6, 1987, in the Daxing'anling Mountains. Forest fires were not new to the region, but this fire was worse than previous blazes. The Daxing'anling Wildfire burned for almost one month. In that time, it scorched 2.4 million acres (971,000 ha), killed more than 200 people, and left 50,000 others homeless.[10]

During a drought in 1989, more than 1,100 wildfires burned more than eight million acres (3 million ha) in Canada.[11] Officials discovered that many of these fires were accidentally started by people. As a result of the blazes, authorities evacuated 24,500 people from 32 towns.[12]

The next decade, Indonesia experienced a major wildfire. The Indonesia Wildfire burned in 1997 and 1998. The blaze was massive, destroying almost 20 million acres

People work to stop a wildfire from spreading to their village in Indonesia in 1998.

(8 million ha) of land.[13] At the time, the blaze was believed to be the biggest forest fire ever recorded. The size would be eclipsed a few years later.

2000s

In 2003 in Russia, Siberia's subarctic forests burned and burned. The wildfires burned 47 million acres (19 million ha).[14] That amount, covering an area roughly the size of South Dakota, made Siberia's fire the largest known wildfire in world history.

That same year, 14 wildfires burned in Southern California in October. One was started by a lost hiker in hopes of alerting rescuers. It became the Cedar Fire and torched approximately 273,000 acres (111,000 ha), including more than 2,000 homes. This was only a fraction of the damage caused by all 14 fires. Before they were extinguished in November, the blazes had consumed more than 750,000 acres (304,000 ha).[15] Fourteen people died.[16]

Mediterranean countries also experience wildfires. In the summer of 2007, Greece had many wildfires. Before the last one was put out, 670,000 acres (271,139 ha) of forest and farmland had burned, and 84 people had died.[17]

In 2009, Australia experienced another massive set of wildfires—the worst at that point in the country's history. On February 7, as many as 400 fires raged in Victoria. The Black Saturday bushfires burned for a month, burning 1.1 million acres (445,000 ha) of land and killing 173 people.[18]

"THE FLAMES WERE HEAD HEIGHT FROM THE GROUND."[19]

—RODNEY LEATHAM, SURVIVOR OF AUSTRALIA'S BLACK SATURDAY BUSHFIRES

2010s

In the 2010s, record-setting wildfires continued to affect lives and make news headlines. In 2011, Texas had its worst fire season to date. More than 31,000 wildfires burned more than four million acres (1.6 million ha). In 2013, the Yarnell Hill Fire in Arizona destroyed more than 8,000 acres (3,200 ha). Nineteen firefighters died battling the blaze. The following year, the

An aerial photo shows just part of the vast area destroyed by the Carlton Complex Fire in Washington State in 2014.

Carlton Complex Fire blazed in Washington State. The July 2014 fire destroyed at least 340 homes and was the largest wildfire in the state's recorded history.[20]

That same year, Canada's Northwest Territories region had its worst fire season in 30 years. More than seven million acres (3 million ha) burned.[21] Smoke and ash reached more than nine miles (15 km) high. The wildfire worsened air quality in parts of Canada and the United States. The smoky air spread as far as Portugal.

These examples from the past several decades show the harm wildfires can cause to nature, homes, and human life. But this sample is only a small portion of what has occurred. Wildfires today, including Australia's 2019–20 bushfires, are changing. Scientists see that wildfires are bigger and more frequent now than in the past.

MORE FIRES, BIGGER FIRES

Wildfires are a natural part of many ecosystems. However, in recent years, wildfires have become stronger and more frequent. Additionally, fires are beginning to burn in areas that previously had few fires. With a warming and drying climate, wildfires have the potential to become bigger. In turn, as the world's population continues to rise, fires will be more and more likely to affect populated areas.

For example, in September 2020, intense wildfires burned across the states of Oregon, Washington, and California. The fires burned millions of acres. More than a dozen people were killed and thousands of others

A firefighter rescues goats from a farm damaged by a wildfire in California. Experts say wildfires are increasingly damaging areas where people live.

evacuated from their homes. Experts linked these blazes to the trend of increasingly destructive wildfires.

THE WESTERN UNITED STATES

Scientists at a NASA-funded project called Rehabilitation Capability Convergence for Ecosystem Recovery (RECOVER) have done extensive research into wildfires in the western United States. Specifically, RECOVER personnel have studied more than 40,000 wildfires from Colorado to California that took place between 1950 and 2017. These researchers wanted to know how wildfire traits have changed over time. The scientists analyzed wildfire data in several states, including

ANIMALS FIGHT FIRES

Animals play a role in making wildfires more or less likely. Goats and cattle can help clear grass. This cuts down on the available fuel, helping with fire management in grassy places. Not allowing grazing can result in hotter and bigger fires and increase the area of land burned.

However, grazing animals can increase the likelihood of a fire when they eat all the plants that are more fire-resistant and leave behind vegetation that is more likely to burn. According to Claire Foster, a terrestrial conservation biologist at Australian National University, "When you take out all the nutritious, palatable plants, those left over tend to be drier and more flammable."[1]

Other animals can help reduce fires because they change the placement of vegetation. Some birds move dried leaves on the ground, and elephants crush the plants they walk on. Both of these things interrupt the path of fuel, which will slow a fire down and may cause it to die out.

The Las Conchas fire in 2011 in New Mexico was considered a megafire. It burned more than 150,000 acres (60,700 ha).

Arizona, California, Colorado, Idaho, Montana, New Mexico, Nevada, Oregon, Washington, and Wyoming.

Six trends emerged. First, the scientists found that more wildfires were happening than in previous years. Since 1950, the number of annual wildfires had grown at a steady pace. Most of the wildfires that had occurred in the past 60 years had been since 2000. Secondly, the size of wildfires had increased. The number of megafires, defined as those which burn more than 100,000 acres (247,000 ha), had grown since 1970.

The third trend observed by RECOVER researchers was that the amount of land in the west that had burned was a small percentage. Even with an increase in fires, the researchers found that only 11 percent of land in the western states had been affected by wildfires since 1950.[2]

FORESTS AFTER A FIRE

After a wildfire, the forest that burned may look quite different than it did before the fire. Some trees may be completely burned. However, other areas may only have light burning. While animals may have fled some areas, they also have new places to shelter. For example, some types of birds and insects thrive by making their homes in burned, dead trees. Additionally, fires bring new growth and nutrients to soil. Heavily burned areas are open. It is easier for predators to find food. Sapling trees thrive in the open areas. It does not take long for a forest to begin to regrow after a fire.

In addition, RECOVER found no pattern to the fires. Rather, they were random, including in terms of whether the land that burned was private or public. Keith Weber of Idaho State University managed the study and was surprised by the low percentage. Weber offered possible reasons for this low figure: "Some of the 89 percent may not burn because it has low susceptibility—not dry enough or it has low fuel (vegetation). Some areas may be really ripe for a fire, but they have not had an ignition source yet."[3] Scientists believe another reason may be human action. People work to keep areas from burning and suppress any small fires that may ignite.

The fourth trend was that wildfires reoccurred in some locations. Fires tend to burn in the same place more than once, which is called reburning. According to RECOVER, approximately 3 percent of land in the western United States had experienced multiple wildfires over time. Some places had up to 11 wildfires, averaging a fire approximately every seven years.[4]

The fifth trend involved the types of plants in wildfires. Scientists found that recent wildfires had burned coniferous forests more than any other vegetation. Conifers are trees that have cones, such as pines, redwoods, and spruces.

And lastly, RECOVER concluded that wildfires will greatly affect the United States in the future. Scientists believe environmental changes will result in a greater increase in very large fires by the middle of the twenty-first century. Very large fires are defined as wildfires that burn more than 50,000 acres (20,000 ha).

WILDFIRES AND WEATHER

Wildfires can create their own weather. The results of this have become more severe as wildfires have become

A pyrocumulus cloud forms above a wildfire in Oregon.

stronger and more intense in recent decades. These weather formations can further increase the damage caused by fires.

Wildfires can create a type of cloud called pyrocumulus, which means "fire cloud." Wildfires force air up, pushing it above the fire. This movement makes the air unstable, which makes the air move upward faster. This process is similar to that in which thunderstorms form. As the air rises, it cools and forms into drops of water on the fires' ash. This creates a cloud. Sometimes, depending on how big a fire is, a pyrocumulonimbus, or "fire storm cloud," will form. These clouds can drop rain. They can also result in dry lightning, which can spark new fires.

Wildfires can create other weather features too. One is wind patterns. Warmer air rises, and the speed of this rise increases with temperature. That means that the air around wildfires rises quickly. The rapid movement pulls in the surrounding air near the fire, creating wind.

This can result in swirling air near the fire, causing a firenado. As its name suggests, a firenado is a fire tornado. Firenados can suck in ash and embers. According to AccuWeather meteorologist Jordan Root, "When wildfires are intense, air tends to move much more violently, producing strong gusts, which creates a chaotic and dangerous environment for firefighters."[5]

"THE NUMBER OF FIRES AND THEIR SIZE VARIES FROM YEAR TO YEAR, BUT THE BIG TREND IS THAT THE RISK OF FIRE IS INCREASING GLOBALLY."[6]

—SUSANNE WINTER, FOREST PROGRAM MANAGER, WORLD WILDLIFE FUND GERMANY

WILDFIRES WORLDWIDE

The recent growth in the number of wildfires extends well beyond the western United States. The number and size of wildfires worldwide has increased. In 2019, the website Global Forest Watch recorded more than 4.5 million fires that were bigger than 256 acres (100 ha). This number was 400,000 more than the total number of wildfires in 2018.[7]

REPLANTING AFTER THE PICKETT FIRE

In 2015, the Pickett Fire in the Shasta-Trinity National Forest in California claimed more than 36,000 acres (15,000 ha). In spring 2018, the US Forest Service replanted 250 acres (100 ha) with 71,250 Douglas fir, ponderosa pine, and sugar pine seedlings.[9] According to the Arbor Day Foundation, which is dedicated to trees, replanting trees after a forest fire is important. Replanting has many positive effects. In addition to helping improve air quality, trees also help improve water quality by acting as filters. Some trees help aquatic habitats by regulating water temperature, which is important for some aquatic animals. Forests also play a role in the landscape. They help minimize floods. Tree roots soak up extra rain, reducing the likelihood of extreme flooding. Forests also serve as homes for wildlife and places for people to enjoy nature.

Africa and South America have both experienced higher numbers of fires. In Africa, several fires have burned from South Sudan to West Africa. In South America, fires in Brazil have burned wide swaths of the Amazon rain forest. In Asia, Indonesia has experienced increasing numbers of fires as well. By the end of September 2019, more than two million acres (8 ha) had burned on the island nation.[8] This was more area than in all of 2018 and the most since 2015.

Fires are also affecting naturally cold areas. In 2019, some areas of the Arctic that have had fires only rarely saw a notable increase in wildfires. In a few weeks in summer 2019, fire burned approximately six million acres (2.4 million ha) in Siberia. That amount of land is approximately the size of Vermont. Also in 2019, Alaska saw 2.5 million acres (1 million ha) of its snow forest and tundra burned by wildfires.[10]

The Arctic is warming faster than any other place on the planet. Its temperatures are increasing twice as fast compared to other regions. One challenge this presents specific to wildfires is lightning. Some researchers have found that warming in the Arctic is causing more lightning, and lightning is a major cause of fires in remote regions, such as Siberia and Alaska.

Wildfires continue to grow in number and size. As a result, scientists continue to study how to prevent and prepare for future fires. Understanding the causes for this change in wildfires is critical. Knowing the causes can help people deal with them.

CHAPTER FIVE

WHY ARE FIRES GETTING WORSE?

Understanding what has made wildfires more intense and more frequent can help people try to prevent them or reduce their damage. The intensity of a fire is measured by how much fuel burns and how quickly. The massive wildfires in California and Australia in the late 2010s brought widespread attention to the devastation that these blazes can cause. They also highlighted the causes of the fires' intensification, including climate change.

Firefighters work to protect a cabin from a 50,000-acre (20,230 ha) wildfire in the Caribou Hills of Alaska.

GLOBAL WARMING VS. CLIMATE CHANGE

People often use the terms *global warming* and *climate change* interchangeably. However, they are not synonymous. Global warming focuses on temperatures and the warming of Earth's climate since the late 1800s, when humans began burning fossil fuels more. Burning these fuels increases the amount of greenhouse gases in Earth's atmosphere. These gases include carbon dioxide, methane, and nitrous oxide. They trap heat, making Earth warmer.

Climate change is broader than global warming. It focuses on more than surface temperature. Climate change also considers ocean temperature, sea level, and glacier size. Climate change takes into account how often weather and climate events occur and their severity. These include droughts, floods, heat waves, hurricanes, and wildfires.

Climate change considers more than the human factor of burning fossil fuels. Nature can also play a role in climate change. Some natural factors that affect the climate include regularly occurring patterns in the planet's oceans, volcanic activity, differences in the amount of energy the sun releases, and changes in Earth's orbit.

CLIMATE CHANGE BASICS

Climate change includes the gradual warming of the planet's average temperatures. It is accelerated by human activity, including the release of gases that trap heat in the atmosphere. Many people pinpoint climate change as one reason for the way wildfires have changed. Understanding climate change is essential to understanding why fires have become more severe and more frequent. It is especially crucial to understand the difference between climate and weather.

Weather is about the short term—what happens in the atmosphere across minutes, hours, and even days. Clouds, rain, snow, and winds are all parts of weather. Climate is about the long term. It is weather averaged over the course of several years. Meteorologists provide forecasts that extend a few days on the nightly news. Climatologists and other researchers seek to predict the conditions on the planet decades into the future.

Researchers use a variety of data to understand climate change, including readings from the ground, the air, and space. NASA is among the government agencies that studies climate. On its website, it explains:

> *Climate data records provide evidence of climate change key indicators, such as global land and ocean temperature increases; rising sea levels; ice loss at Earth's poles and in mountain glaciers; frequency and severity changes in extreme weather such as hurricanes, heatwaves, wildfires, droughts, floods, and precipitation; and cloud and vegetation cover changes, to name but a few.*[1]

CALIFORNIA HEAT

California's eastern Santa Ana winds are a major factor in the state's wildfires. The Santa Ana winds form over the Great Basin, an area of the western United States that includes eastern California. The winds are hot and dry. They move toward the coast of Southern California after the area's dry season. These hot winds intensify the conditions for wildfires. Additionally, California has experienced hotter temperatures as a result of climate change. Higher temperatures can help drive wildfires. California's 2017 wildfire season was its most expensive and most destructive on record. Six of the state's ten biggest fires happened in the 2010s.[2]

> "CLIMATE IS REALLY RUNNING THE SHOW IN TERMS OF WHAT BURNS. WE SHOULD BE GETTING READY FOR BIGGER FIRE YEARS THAN THOSE FAMILIAR TO PREVIOUS GENERATIONS."[3]
>
> **—PARK WILLIAMS, PROFESSOR OF BIOLOGY AND ENVIRONMENT, COLUMBIA UNIVERSITY**

Park Williams, a professor of biology and environment at Columbia University, studied data in California and discovered that spring rainfall amounts were typical in 2018 and higher than usual in 2017. This healthy amount of rain suggests that the wildfire seasons in those years would have been unremarkable. But the opposite occurred because of increased heat. "Last year and this year we've seen giant outbreaks of fires in areas where you wouldn't have expected it based on the soil-moisture balance [from the rain]," Williams explained to the *Atlantic* magazine in summer 2018. Williams went on to explain:

> *The factor that clearly made the difference in 2017, and again in 2018, is heat. Last summer was record-breaking, or near record-breaking, hot across much of the West, and I believe July 2018 will break records or come close to it again this year. Even if the deep soils are wet following winter and spring, a hot and dry atmosphere seems to be able to overwhelm that effect.*[4]

CALIFORNIA'S NEW NORMAL

As Americans looked forward to celebrating Independence Day in 2018, firefighters across the western United States battled wildfires. Blazes burned in California, Colorado, New Mexico, and other places. Fire captain Mark Bailey battled a wildfire in Guinda, California. He assessed the situation in his state: "The fields dried out quickly. A big fire like this in early July is the new normal for California." Chris Anthony, a division chief at Cal Fire, echoed Bailey. Anthony said, "We shouldn't be seeing this type of fire behavior this early in the year. It really speaks to the fact that in California and in [the western states] in general, fires are burning, and they are behaving differently from what we've seen them do in the past."[5]

Research suggests that temperature and humidity have a greater effect on wildfires than moisture in the soil. This is bad news, Williams explained, because Earth is getting warmer as part of climate change. July 2018 was California's hottest month ever recorded up to that point. The difference was significant—five degrees Fahrenheit (9°C) hotter than

A firefighter holds a hose while helping battle a wildfire in Santa Rosa, California, in 2017.

usual.[6] In the western United States, 17 of the 18 warmest years on record have been since 2001.[7]

According to the California Department of Forestry and Fire Protection (Cal Fire), 14 of the state's biggest fires have burned since 2000. LeRoy Westerling is codirector of the Center for Climate Communication at the University of California–Merced and has been studying climate change since 1999. He said of California's wildfires, "Wildfire is a competition of climate, people, and ecosystems, and each one has complex interactions with non-linear results. Put it all together, add in the extra heat, and you get really uncharacteristic, really dangerous fire behavior."[8]

WILDFIRES IN CANADA

Authorities in Canada have also discussed climate and wildfires in their country. Some have compared Canada to Australia. "What's happening in Australia now is extraordinary," said Ed Struzik, a fellow at the Institute for Energy and Environmental Policy at Canada's Queen's University, in January 2020. "We're as vulnerable as any country in the world," he added.[9]

In 2017 and 2018, British Columbia, Canada's westernmost province, declared a state of emergency. Both years set records for wildfires. Canada has a considerable amount of wildland. Approximately 33 percent of the world's forests are in Canada.[10] According to Struzik, Canada's potential for wildfire is increasing as a result of climate change and an abundance of fuel. Some of this fuel is created by insects such as the mountain pine beetle, which kills trees. The dead trees dry out and serve as fuel for wildfires. "The signals are there," Struzik said,

"IT'S A WARMER WORLD AND PART OF A WARMER WORLD IS MORE FIRE."[11]

—MIKE FLANNIGAN, WILDLAND FIRE PROFESSOR, UNIVERSITY OF ALBERTA

MORE TO THE STORY

MOUNTAIN PINE BEETLES

The mountain pine beetle, or bark beetle, has played a role in North America's evergreen forests for millennia. The beetle is approximately the size of a grain of rice. Bark beetles usually attack and kill trees that are old, sick, or suffering from drought or physical damage. To infect a tree, bark beetles lay eggs in the tree that hatch into larvae that feed on the tree. Healthy trees create a resin that wards off infestation. Weak trees cannot defend themselves against insects the way healthy trees can. Occasional outbreaks of the bug result in the loss of millions of trees, wiping out chunks of forest. This led some residents of areas affected by bark beetles to believe the insects were responsible for an increase in wildfires.

However, in 2013, a group of US researchers studied bark beetle outbreaks in relation to wildfires in the Rocky Mountains. They concluded that although bark beetles do help create fuel for fires, these insects are not a primary cause of increased wildfire risk, compared to other factors. The researchers wrote, "Outbreaks of mountain pine beetle . . . do not appear to substantially increase the risk of subsequent fire under most conditions. Instead, fire risk . . . is strongly tied to warm and dry conditions, such as those of recent decades. As long as the severe droughts we have been seeing in recent years persist, we can expect a high risk of fire—regardless of beetle outbreaks."[12]

"very strong signals that we're going to see things get a lot worse before they get better."[13]

Mike Flannigan, a wildland fire professor at the University of Alberta in Canada, is also concerned about climate change and how it will affect wildfires in his country as it has in Australia. "The warmer it is, the longer the fire season," he said. "The warmer it is, the more lightning you see."[14] According to Flannigan, a 1.8-degrees-Fahrenheit (1°C) jump increases the number of lightning strikes by approximately 12 percent. Lightning sparks more than 50 percent of Canada's wildfires.

RUSSIA'S WORST FIRES

Boreal forests are forests that grow in the subarctic regions of the world. Russia is home to the world's largest boreal forest. Russians use the term *taiga* for these forests. The word translates in English to "land of the little sticks." Taigas are also found in other places on Earth, including Alaska, Canada, and Scandinavia. Russia's taiga spans from the Pacific Ocean to the Ural Mountains, stretching approximately 3,600 miles (5,800 km).

August 2019 was particularly bad for fires in Russia's taiga. Earlier that summer, in June and July, scientists recorded the hottest average global temperatures in documented history up to that point. Siberia, which is known for its frigid temperatures, was ten degrees Fahrenheit (6°C) warmer than the average from 1981 to 2010.[15] The higher temperature led to dry conditions that made wildfires more likely. The result was that the world's largest forest had multiple fires. In addition, officials waited for several months for rain to extinguish the blaze without success.

BURNING FOR AGRICULTURE

Climate change is not the only factor in the wildfire equation. Sometimes, people set fires deliberately. Prescribed burns to clear land happen with great frequency over vast areas. Prescribed burns may be used for ecosystem health. But people also use prescribed burns to quickly clear areas for agriculture.

In Africa, several wildfires have burned from South Sudan to West Africa. Many people live in the affected areas. According to Susanne Winter, who manages the

World Wildlife Fund's forest program, "Landowners and farmers [use fire to clear] their fields to quickly get rid of vegetation and make the soil fertile in the short term."[16] These people, however, sometimes lose control of the fires.

South America has had increasing numbers of fires as humans continue to burn the Amazon, clearing the land so farmers can use it for crops. In 2019, South America had more fires than its total number of fires between 2010 and 2018. Using fire to clear land is not new in the Amazon. Indigenous people have cleared patches of the rain forest for countless decades. However, as *New York Times* reporter Kendra Pierre-Louis explained in August 2019, "[Indigenous people] tend to cultivate much smaller areas, plant a relatively diverse number of crops, and move onto a new plot of land after a few years, allowing the forest

INDIAN OCEAN DIPOLE

The Indian Ocean dipole is a weather pattern that happens in the Indian Ocean. It affects weather in Australia, among other places. A positive dipole occurs when the eastern Indian Ocean is cooler than normal and the western portion is warmer than normal. Experts have found a correlation between strong positive dipoles and some of Australia's worst bushfire seasons. In 2019, the Indian Ocean dipole was in an especially strong positive phase—the strongest in more than 20 years. As a result, moisture moved west, to eastern Africa, leaving Australia and Indonesia with a lack of rain. The lack of moisture and hotter air temperatures made the 2019 bushfire season one of Australia's worst on record.

to regrow."[17] By contrast, the burning in recent years is for agriculture that is more industrialized, usually resulting in a permanent loss of trees.

In Asia, people have burned millions of acres of forest intentionally. The paper and palm oil industries have used up more than 67 million acres (27 million ha) of forest in Indonesia.[18] Southeast Asia has also experienced extensive prescribed burning to make way for palm oil production. Borneo, Malaysia, and Sumatra lost 71 percent of their peat forests between 1990 and 2015, often for this reason.[19]

Experts say people are building homes closer to fire-prone areas, which can be dangerous.

BUILDING IN FIRE-PRONE AREAS

Another way humans are a factor in the wildfire equation is through development. People build houses and live in fire-prone areas. In the United States, people have continued to expand their areas of construction and development, building houses closer and closer to forests. Areas between wildlands and cities had 12.7 million more houses and 25 million more people added between 1990 and 2010.[20] In 2019, approximately four million homes in California were in locations that could put them in harm's way as a result of wildfires.[21]

People live in wildfire-prone areas for different reasons. Some may want to be closer nature. Rural areas tend to be less expensive than urban ones, so some people may live in these areas to have lower living expenses. Still others work in the area, perhaps in agriculture or timber, and want to live conveniently close to their work. The increase of homes being built in these areas is also a result of population growth—development expands as more people need places to live. Increasing numbers of Americans are living in houses that have been built in forests. Jessica Gardetto of the National Interagency Fire Center, located in Boise, Idaho, spoke with the *New York Times* about the threat this causes for these residents. "It's not a matter of if a wildfire is going to come to your home—it's a matter of when," she said.[22]

The risk of living in fire-prone areas is illustrated by past wildfires that have caused death and destruction. One of the many wildfires in California in 2018 was the Camp Fire. It became the deadliest fire in the state's history, wiping out the town of Paradise and killing dozens of residents.

THE ROLE OF ELECTRICITY

Another factor, at least in some instances, is electricity. Specifically, electrical lines and equipment can ignite wildfires when electrical lines come in contact with vegetation.

High winds may blow branches onto power lines. The lines may spark and start a fire. In other instances, storms may cause power lines to fall and ignite brush on the ground. Electricity-related causes account for 10 percent of California's wildfires.[23] The state has thousands of

Electrical lines are some of the things built by humans that can cause wildfires.

miles of electrical lines. Three utility companies dominate California's electricity landscape. Pacific Gas and Electric (PG&E), Southern California Edison, and San Diego Gas and Electric maintain almost 250,000 miles (402,000 km) of power lines in California that provide power to approximately 22 million people.[24]

Climate change, human actions, and electricity contribute to the increase in wildfires. Forest management practices may lead to an increase in fire-prone vegetation and fuels. Scientists study these factors. By gaining more complete information, government agencies and other organizations can strategize effective ways to limit wildfires. Limiting wildfires not only protects human property but also protects valuable wild habitats for plants and animals.

FROM THE HEADLINES

THE CAMP FIRE

The blaze that became known as the Camp Fire began early on November 8, 2018, in the foothills of the Sierra Nevada in Northern California, near the town of Paradise. Sparks from power lines almost 100 years old started the fire along Camp Creek Road. The blaze burned for 17 days. At its peak, the fire spread at a rate equivalent to 80 football fields per minute. In the second week of the blaze, more than 5,000 firefighters worked to contain it. They came from across the state and the country.

The Camp Fire caused massive damage. The blaze scorched 153,335 acres (62,052 ha) of land and destroyed 18,800 buildings, including almost 14,000 homes. Eighty-five people died.[25] Some of them were in vehicles and trying to escape.

Perhaps the most striking image of the fire was the loss of Paradise. On the wildfire's first day of burning, it tore through the town. In four hours, the fire essentially destroyed Paradise. When it was done burning, the Camp Fire had become California's most destructive and deadliest wildfire. President Donald Trump later visited what was left

President Donald Trump, *center*, visited the wreckage in the aftermath of the Camp Fire.

of Paradise. He expressed a desire to see an end to destructive wildfires. "I think, hopefully, this will be the last of these," he said.[26]

In June 2020, the CEO of PG&E, the owner of the power lines, pleaded guilty to 84 counts of manslaughter. The court case determined that the fire was a direct result of PG&E's failure to maintain one of its lines. PG&E will pay $13.5 billion to people who lost their homes and businesses due to its negligence.

CHAPTER SIX

THE COSTS OF WILDFIRES

As example after example has shown, wildfires come with high costs to human life. They are costly in different ways. One element of wildfire damage is financial costs. These costs take different forms, such as losing a house and having to buy a new home or rebuild. Even having to repair a house that was partially damaged by fire can be very expensive. According to the California Department of Insurance, homeowners, renters, and business owners claimed more than $10 billion in losses in 2018 and 2019 as a result of wildfires.[1]

Another financial cost is insurance, at least in areas that tend to have wildfires. In these regions, the cost for home insurance has been rising. This means that people

Thousands of Californians have lost their homes to wildfires.

who live in these areas, even if they have not experienced a fire themselves, pay more for their insurance. The Rand Corporation, a nonprofit research organization in the state, studied insurance in specific areas of California. A review of average premiums, or monthly insurance payments, in two areas with a high risk for wildfires saw a similar pattern between 2007 and 2014. The high-risk part of the Sierra Foothills had an increase of 12 percent, and the high-risk area of San Bernardino County had an increase of 15 percent. This trend will likely continue. Rand's study, published in 2018, projected that homeowners in areas with the greatest risk for wildfires will pay 18 percent more for home insurance by 2055.[2]

"OUR DEVELOPMENT PATTERNS HAVE INCREASED THE ENCOUNTERS OF WHERE HUMANS ARE LIVING NOW AND WHERE WILDFIRES ARE OCCURRING."[4]

—KIMIKO BARRETT, POLICY AND RESEARCH ANALYST

Another financial cost is firefighting expenses. In 2017, the US Forest Service spent almost $3 billion fighting wildfires across the United States. That amount was more than $2 billion higher than 2015, and it accounted for more than half the agency's budget for the year.[3] The more money that goes to firefighting, the less money there is for other activities, such as forest management, which can help mitigate wildfires.

State governments also spend money fighting fires. In several western states, the government employs firefighters. Some are employed through the state Department of Natural Resources, such as in Washington. These firefighters are responsible for containing and suppressing wildfires in the state.

California has one of the largest fire budgets in the nation. In 2018, Cal Fire spent $1 billion doing its work. In addition, the state had another record year in damages from wildfires, which totaled $400 billion.[5]

Other nations have tallied losses as well. Indonesia's government estimated its economic losses at as high as $30 billion as a result of fires in 2016.[6] And economists in Australia have estimated $100 billion in losses there as a result of the 2019–20 bushfires.[7] The number makes the fires Australia's most expensive natural disaster ever.

HEALTH COSTS

As Australia's 2019–20 bushfires have shown, wildfires threaten public health. They can cause tremendous harm to people, including death. One cause of death from wildfires is being trapped and burned. Wildfire smoke can also be deadly. Smoke has tiny particles that can cause minor to severe physical aggravation. Less-severe symptoms include burning eyes and a runny nose. For people with lung or heart diseases, wildfire smoke can make breathing difficult, even to the point of causing death. In 2015, the burning of peat in Southeast Asia caused smog and haze that were so heavy they may have resulted in the premature deaths of more than 100,000 people.[8]

WILDFIRES AND NATIONAL SECURITY

Wildfires become even more threatening when they encroach on military installations, which store explosives and chemicals. Personnel at Vandenberg Air Force Base in California learned this firsthand in September 2016 when a fire burned 12,000 acres (4,856 ha) of the base's land. Fortunately, crews put out the fire without any further problems. However, the incident highlights concerns expressed in a 2019 report by the US Department of Defense (DOD). The DOD analyzed threats related to climate change—for example, droughts, flooding, and wildfires—at 72 US military bases worldwide. The DOD stated, "The effects of a changing climate are a national security issue." According to the DOD, wildfires are an issue for approximately 50 percent of the bases, and the department believed the list would grow by seven bases in the next two decades.[9] As a result, military bases have made plans to clear brush in order to reduce the risk of fire.

Australia's 2019–20 wildfires showed how much smoke can spread. The smoke on January 1, 2020, was so thick that satellite images could not differentiate between land

People wear face masks in 2019 in San Francisco, California, to protect themselves from wildfire smoke in the air.

and water in some areas. They could see only smoke. The National Oceanic and Atmospheric Administration (NOAA) reported that wind had pushed Australia's wildfire smoke over South America and that the smoke was "in the process of circumnavigating the planet."[10]

Wildfires also affect another aspect of human health. They can cause tremendous stress and have long-lasting effects on mental health. People faced with wildfires face evacuation and the threat of losing their homes, belongings, pets, and loved ones. A wildfire may burn down one home, 100 homes, or whole communities. A fire can destroy an entire neighborhood or town.

CLIMATE COSTS

Wildfires may also affect the climate. They add to a cycle. For example, climate change has made bushfires in

Australia more likely and more severe. In turn, the fires add to climate change. As trees burn, the smoke and ash add carbon dioxide to the atmosphere.

An additional issue is that extinguishing a fire does not stop its carbon emissions. According to researchers at Oregon State University, a tree releases approximately 15 percent of its carbon during a fire. Another 35 percent enters the air over the next 50 years. Finally, it takes another 50 years—100 years after the fire—to emit the remaining 50 percent of the carbon.[11]

These many costs highlight the importance of controlling wildfires. Firefighters aim to do just that, using several approaches in their work. Controlling and preventing wildfires can reduce damage to towns and save lives.

CARBON SINKS

One challenge created by the loss of forests is that forests are carbon sinks. A carbon sink is a natural feature that takes in carbon dioxide from the atmosphere, just as a sponge or paper towel soaks up water. More specifically, a carbon sink takes in more carbon than it releases. Plants, oceans, and soil are all carbon sinks, and they absorb some of the gases that are causing climate change, such as carbon dioxide. Together, the land and ocean carbon sinks take in approximately 50 percent of human carbon dioxide emissions.

MORE TO THE STORY

PYROPHYTIC PLANTS

Not all plants suffer from wildfires. Types of plants called pyrophytes have adapted over time to withstand fire. In some instances, fire helps them. One adaptation is developing seeds that sprout in response to fire. Plants such as the lodgepole pine have cones or fruits that open only after the heat from a fire melts the resin that covers them. Other plants with fire-activated seeds respond to the smoke and burned vegetation caused by a fire.

Insulation is another adaptation. Giant sequoias have bark that is particularly thick as well as fire-retardant. The mighty trees can withstand being burned to some extent. And a type of bush called a protea has a layer of moist tissue that serves as insulation and prevents the plant from drying out.

Still other plants have adapted by resprouting after being burned. Some types of eucalyptus do this, sending out buds that will become new branches and leaves. Flowering is also an adaptation. After a fire, plants such as the Australian grass tree send out numerous buds that result in an abundance of flowers.

Some trees have adapted by changing their shapes. These plants have few or no lower branches. Instead, the growth is at the top of the trunk, which gives them tall crowns. This adaptation limits damage from wildfires.

CHAPTER SEVEN

FIGHTING WILDFIRES

Fighting wildfires is important because of the harm they can cause. Firefighters battle these blazes in different ways. They increasingly rely on technology to detect and stop wildfires. As wildfires grow in intensity and frequency around the world, people must continue finding ways to fight them.

ON THE GROUND

The people who fight wildfires on the ground have various roles. Hand crews are teams of approximately 20 firefighters. They use hand tools to establish a fire line, which is also called a firebreak. This is an area with all the fire fuels removed. This strip of cleared land is supposed to stop the wildfire from spreading.

A fire crew works to put out the White Draw Fire, a 5,000-acre (2,020 ha) wildfire in South Dakota in 2012.

342
E34
McKIE

When creating a fire line, firefighters use a type of ax called a Pulaski for chopping, trenching, and grubbing, which is digging up roots.

These firefighters battle wildfires in other ways too. They keep an eye on areas that have not burned to ensure no sparks or embers cross the fire line. They check on areas where the fire has been contained, verifying the fire has been put out completely. Firefighters on the ground also spray water and fire retardant on flames. The chemical slows the fire and cools it. Fire is another tool in the firefighting arsenal. Firefighters set backfires, which are intentional fires that move toward the wildfire. Backfires burn up the fuels that would feed the wildfire.

Firefighters working on hand crews often battle wildfires in 12-hour shifts. Hotshot crews are the hand crews with the most experience. These firefighters tackle the toughest fires and wildfires in challenging areas, such as remote or rugged terrain.

Bulldozer or tractor-plow crews also battle wildfires on the ground. These crews have three to five firefighters. They operate bulldozers and tractor plows, using this heavy equipment to create fire lines.

While working on the ground, firefighters have to get up close to the flames and smoke.

Engine crews also work with heavy equipment—in this case, fire engines. A fire engine holds 250 to 750 gallons (946 to 2,839 L) of water. These crews have three to five members. Engine crews handle heavy fire hoses that are several hundred feet long.

Smoke jumpers are firefighters who parachute into areas of wildfires that are difficult to access by land. They also go to areas with small fires to fight them and keep them from growing into large blazes. Smoke jumpers fight fires using the same methods as hand crews.

Because fighting wildfires is risky, firefighters rely on protective gear and equipment. For example, they wear fire-resistant clothes. They also rely on fire shelters. These are portable, tentlike structures covered with aluminum, measuring seven feet (2.1 m) long, four feet (1.2 m) wide, and two feet (0.6 m) high. The shelter reflects heat and provides breathable air inside for firefighters. Firefighters enter these shelters as the last option when trapped in a fire.

FIGHTING FIRES FROM THE AIR AT NIGHT

New technology allows firefighters to work at night. In the past, it was too dangerous to fly helicopters at night. But as night vision goggles became more advanced, it became easier for pilots to fly. Fighting fires at night has several benefits. One is that winds are often less strong. Firefighters can get closer to the flames. They use their helicopters to dump water or retardant on the fires. Another benefit is that the air temperature cools at night. The air has more moisture. Because of the increased humidity, water and fire retardant are more effective.

FROM THE AIR

Firefighters also attack fires from the air. In addition to transporting firefighters to hard-to-reach areas, helicopters carry buckets of water, foam, or fire retardant to drop on or near the fire. A Bambi bucket is collapsible and hangs from a helicopter. The pilot fills the bucket by dropping it into a lake or other water source and drops the water on the fire. A bucket can hold hundreds of gallons of water.

Air tankers can drop considerably more firefighting material. Air tankers are planes fitted with tanks that carry thousands of gallons of water or retardant. Pilots drop the

A helicopter drops water over a wildfire in Utah.

loads ahead of a wildfire to keep the fire from advancing. Air tankers can make a big difference in battling a wildfire. An analysis of US Forest Service data showed that when air tankers responded within an hour, the average duration of a blaze was 29 minutes. When they took more than three days to respond, that average duration grew to almost two weeks.[1]

FIGHTING FIRES WITH TECHNOLOGY

Technology also plays a role in firefighting. For example, some aircraft have special equipment to collect heat data. This information can tell firefighters where wildfires are burning at the moment and where they might pop up.

Firefighters use drones too. These remotely piloted aircraft can gather heat data. Drones are better suited for observing grassland fires than forest fires. The reason is that forest fires burn hotter and are erratic compared to grassland fires. The person operating the drone needs to be nearby, making unpredictable fires more dangerous for the operator.

Farther up in the sky, satellites controlled by NASA and NOAA gather other useful information. They collect data about wind speed and direction and about the dryness of the land around a fire. This information can help firefighters predict how quickly and where a fire will spread.

ALERT WILDLIFE

California is focused on using technology to provide the best possible outcome regarding wildfires. The University of California, San Diego, operates ALERT Wildlife in conjunction with the University of Nevada and the University of Oregon. ALERT is a system of approximately 300 high-definition cameras focused on areas that have a high risk for fire. The cameras have a long range, seeing as far as 70 miles (113 km) during the day and 100 miles (161 km) at night. The cameras move every two minutes, taking in imagery that goes into a computer. That computer establishes what it sees as the normal conditions for the area in question. Then, when a camera identifies something that is not part of the normal conditions, such as smoke, ALERT sounds an alarm that notifies various local and state authorities. When a fire is detected, the cameras can help pinpoint its exact location.

COMPUTER MODELING

Researchers in Australia and the United States have been working on computer programs to fight wildfires. Phoenix

RapidFire is a computer program that simulates the spread of fire in a chosen area. Australia has been using Phoenix to predict fire behavior in NSW and Victoria for several years. The United States has a similar program called FarSite.

"WE CANNOT JUST ACCEPT DEVASTATING WILDFIRES AS THE 'NEW NORMAL.' CALIFORNIA IS THE GLOBAL LEADER IN TECHNOLOGY AND INNOVATION. WE CAN DEVELOP GAME-CHANGING SOLUTIONS AND GET AHEAD OF THIS PROBLEM."[2]

—MICHAEL PICKER, PRESIDENT, CALIFORNIA PUBLIC UTILITIES COMMISSION

In addition, researchers at the University of Melbourne Bushfire Behavior and Management group have created their own fire-management technology. They designed the Fire Regimen Operations Simulation Tool (FROST) to forecast fire behavior into the next 100 years. FROST will make predictions based on vegetation and how it changes after being burned. Forecasts from FROST can help scientists create plans to protect particular wildlife or plant species within a fire-prone area. Researchers began testing of the technology in 2020.

FROM THE HEADLINES

SHARED FIREFIGHTING

Nations in the Northern and Southern Hemispheres have often shared firefighting information and resources, including air tankers. This has worked well because the two hemispheres have different wildfire seasons. In 2019, Australia leased ten air tankers from the United States. During the 2019–20 bushfire season, firefighting aircraft made almost 40,000 flights over southeastern Australia.

However, this sharing of resources may soon become more difficult. As wildfires continue to grow in strength and number, wildfire seasons will likely overlap. Mira Rojanasakul and Haley Warren of the news website *Bloomberg* wrote, "Climate change is contributing to longer fire seasons and more dangerous conditions, straining this global arrangement and forcing governments and fire services to take drastic action and rethink how fires are fought." In 2019, a group of 23 former fire chiefs and senior officials in Australia wrote to the government about the problem of longer fire seasons and a lack of resources, saying, "The increasing overlap of fire seasons between states and territories and with the USA and Canada will limit our ability to help each other during major emergencies."[3]

After traveling to Australia to help fight wildfires, an American firefighter hugs his daughter upon returning home in February 2020.

PREVENTION

Fires can be devastating to people. But wildfires can also teach people. Lessons learned from these fires inform people about prevention and preparation in different ways. Examples include best practices for campfire safety, building development, and fire management. Legislation is also part of preventing devastating wildfires.

CAMPFIRE SAFETY

Most wildfires are caused by humans, and practicing campfire safety can help prevent many of them. For example, when camping, people should pay attention to fire conditions. Once the campfire is burning, people must pay attention to what is around and make sure the fire doesn't burn out of control.

Researchers study the land after wildfires to learn about how the fires affect the environment. They also study how large wildfires can be managed.

When campers are done with a fire, they must make sure the fire is fully extinguished. The smoldering remains of a campfire can grow into a big wildfire. A good way to make sure a fire is extinguished is by burning the wood completely to ash. Next, pour water on the fire until every ember is soaked and the hissing sound stops. Then, using a shovel, stir the ashes and embers, being sure that none of them are exposed to the air and smoldering. If water is not available, use dirt or sand. Mix the material into the embers. Whether using water, dirt, or sand, keep adding and mixing it into the fire until the fire material is cool.

A DIFFERENT BUILDING APPROACH

Building in or near known wildfire areas puts homes and people at risk. But the practice shows no signs of changing. Therefore, finding a different approach to building could make a difference, and people have made efforts to do that. In California, a 1991 law requires houses, including roofs, to be built with noncombustible materials. A challenge is that that these building codes only apply to construction since 1991, and many houses in California were built before then.

Max Moritz teaches at the Bren School of Environmental Science and Management at the University of California, Santa Barbara. He discussed this issue with the *New York Times* in late 2018. "What we don't have is retrofit programs," he said, referring to programs that would require updating old homes to meet new standards for wildfire safety. "We retrofit for earthquake safety. And there's public funding for mitigating flood exposure. But we don't do that for fire," he said.[1]

The United States could also examine and possibly copy Australia's efforts in the wake of the 2009 Black Saturday bushfires. Australia's government took a multistep approach in an attempt to keep people safe from future

HOUSE SAFETY

People who live in wildfire-prone areas should be mindful of their actions and their environment. There are precautions people can take to not spark a fire and to protect their houses. For example, when cleaning a fireplace, just as with a campfire, they can pour water on the ash and briquettes. Before cutting grass, they should check the fire conditions. A lawn mower could spark a fire.

To protect a house, residents can create a buffer zone of at least 30 feet (9 m). They can take steps to make this area fire-resistant. Plants such as bugleweed, lilacs, lily of the valley, and periwinkle are fire-resistant. Other good options are a green yard—that is, one that is not brown and dry—or a rock garden. And residents can also keep an eye out for forest fuels, such as leaves. They can pile up on the ground, on the roof, and in rain gutters. Finally, firefighting equipment, such as fire extinguishers, should be placed in locations that are easy to access.

wildfires. Steps included identifying places that are prone to bushfires, establishing guidelines to avoid development in those areas, and creating a program to buy land from residents to get them to move to safer locations. In addition, the government revised its bushfire warning system so that it promotes evacuating early rather than staying put and attempting to save a home or property.

PRESCRIBED BURNS

One way fire experts practice wildfire prevention is by using fire. They use prescribed burning to cut back on the amount of brush, trees, and other fire fuels in a specific location. The practice is not a new idea in fire

Firefighters in Australia watch a wallaby run away from the flames as they battle a wildfire.

management. Indigenous peoples such as the Hupa, Miwok, and Chumash communities practiced prescribed burns in current-day California for more than 13,000 years.[2] The US Forest Service began using prescribed burns in the 1940s. According to the Smokey Bear Wildfire Prevention campaign, which is part of the US Forest Service, "Prescribed fire is one of the most effective tools we have in preventing wildfires and managing the intensity and spread of wildfires."[3]

Today, the US government continues to use this practice of prescribed burning, as do several states and some environmental organizations, such as The Nature Conservancy. Florida is one state that uses prescribed burns for fire management. Florida intentionally burns more than 3,280 square miles (8,500 sq km) of its territory each year, which is more than 5 percent of the state.[4] Prescribed burns are not without challenges. High winds can cause fires to burn more quickly or hotter than anticipated. Anyone who uses prescribed burning takes as many safety precautions as possible to keep the fire under control.

DOUBTS ABOUT PRESCRIBED BURNS

Not everyone agrees that prescribed burns are beneficial. Some scientists have questioned the prescribed burns used by experts such as the US Forest Service. Specifically, some ecologists and environmentalists, such as William Baker, a fire and landscape ecologist at the University of Wyoming, have argued that smaller fires such as those used in prescribed burns do not prevent bigger fires. Some believe in letting forest fires burn freely to support natural ecosystems. Several types of forests and ecosystems rely on major fires for biodiversity.

WILDFIRE LEGISLATION

There are many laws regarding wildfires. In Australia, for example, state legislation by Queensland and the Northern and Western Territories created a government group that would be responsible for offering guidance on fire management.

In the United States, California has many laws that address wildfire, 22 of which were established in 2019. Several of those laws focus on the state's power companies. These utility-specific laws require the state's three biggest utility companies to spend a combined total of $5 billion to improve safety and standards. These standards include proper clearing of brush from around power and other utility lines. When California governor Gavin Newsom signed the 22 bills into law in early October 2019, he was positive about the change but was clear that more was needed.

He said, "Given the realities of climate change and extreme weather events, the work is not done, but these bills represent important steps forward on prevention, community resilience, and utility oversight."[5]

PREVENTION CHALLENGES

Fire historian Stephen Pyne told *USA Today* in 2018 that he believes the United States needs to use prescribed burns much more than it does. But Pyne also explained the challenge of this approach to fire prevention: "Prescribed burns are sort of like training a grizzly bear to dance. You can do it, but you never know when he could turn on you."[6]

The city of Mobile, Alabama, experienced this in early 2020. On April 16, the Alabama Forestry Commission started a fire to burn vegetation on 250 acres (101 ha). The blaze quickly got out of control, and several groups of firefighters worked to help contain the fire. The next day, numerous spots were still burning. The fire ultimately burned 180 acres (73 ha) more than planned.[7]

Another point of debate regarding prescribed burns is quantity. Like Florida, California uses prescribed burning

MORE TO THE STORY

THE NATURE CONSERVANCY

The Nature Conservancy (TNC) is a nonprofit organization devoted to helping the environment worldwide. TNC supports prescribed burning because of its importance to the environment and people. Marek Smith, TNC's North America Fire Initiative director, said, "Fire is a global conservation issue. As TNC evolves to address critical threats to life on our planet, our approach aims to help people live with fire, rather than fighting it at every turn." TNC completed its first prescribed burn in 1962. Today, the organization works with areas around the world, including Africa, Australia, Latin America, and the United States.

TNC's fire efforts have changed over the decades from a single focus on managing preserves to one that is multifaceted. According to its website, TNC's work today "includes policy and finance, elevating the contributions of tribes and other indigenous peoples, growing skilled and diverse management workforces, and helping communities develop ways to live more safely with wildfire."[8]

to help prevent wildfires. However, the amount burned is relatively small—31 square miles (80 sq km). Some state officials say California should be using prescribed burning more. Ted Gaines, a state senator, shared with *USA Today* in 2018, "We're really behind the curve. We have clogged forests, which combined with drought conditions, are creating a powder keg."[9] Part of the issue is how the California Environmental Quality Act relates to prescribed burns. This broad state law provides guidelines for permits and projects in relation to protecting the environment. The law "requires state and local agencies to identify the significant environmental impacts of their actions and to avoid or mitigate those impacts, if feasible."[10] This can slow the process of getting approval for a prescribed burn. It can take many months and even up to a year.

Comparatively, Florida's approval time is less than a week. However, Florida and California have very different climates. Florida is humid. The state has a rainy season from May to October that helps control fires. In California, however, the land is dry. A combination of dry plants and invasive grasses in the state means it is potentially more dangerous to start a prescribed burn. California's climate, including poor air quality, also makes officials less flexible in their decision-making. Smoke from prescribed burns adds more pollution to the air. California officials want to limit how much smoke gets into the air.

At the national level, the US Forest Service has struggled to meet its goal of limiting forest fuels through prescribed burns. But even with more funding, prescribed burning would not be enough. In 2018, the *Guardian* reported, "The US Forest Service has said, however, that fuel reduction activities aren't sufficient to keep pace with the changes under way due to climate change."[11]

Stephen Strader, an assistant professor of physical and environmental geography at Villanova University, has

Firefighters work to extinguish a wildfire in the desert near Palmdale, California.

studied the relationship between population and wildfires in the western United States between 1940 and 2010. He found that the population growth in wildfire-prone areas in California, Idaho, Nevada, Oregon, and Washington has exploded, with the number of houses in these places growing from 607,000 to 6.7 million. At the same time, the number of wildfires has grown. Strader explained the challenge of the situation:

> *There is no magic bullet to fix this issue. There needs to be locally driven fire programs, new building codes, and more resilient homes. We sit idly by, time and time again, and we get disaster amnesia. We have to take some responsibility and think more about the risk of buying a home in a wildfire-prone area, just like we need to think about the flooding risk on the coasts.*[12]

COMBATING CLIMATE CHANGE

With research tying increases in wildfire frequency and intensity to climate change, experts argue that fighting climate change is an effective strategy for limiting wildfires. In January 2020, Alice C. Hill of the Council on Foreign Relations wrote about Australia's wildfires and what its government should do to prepare for future fires. In her article, Hill also wrote about the United States.

FROM THE HEADLINES

SHUTTING DOWN POWER TO PREVENT WILDFIRES

In October 2019, millions of people in Northern and central California went without power for a weekend. The outage affected almost one million homes and businesses, and it was not an accident. PG&E, one of California's three major utility providers, shut down power intentionally. It conducted a public safety power shutoff (PSPS) as a precaution during fire-prone weather. Jennifer Robison, PG&E's spokesperson, explained the company's decision: "While we recognize that the scope of these events is unsustainable in the long term, it was the correct decision given the large-scale, historic weather event and ensuing equipment damage that unfolded across our service area."[13]

Members of the California Public Utilities Commission (CPUC) were not pleased with PG&E's decision because frequent power outages are inconvenient for California residents. The commission decided to investigate all such instances of public safety power shutoffs that happened in

A wildfire burns near power lines in California in 2017.

2019 to determine whether PG&E and other utility companies were following established rules and regulations.

Gavin Newsom, California's governor, was also frustrated by PG&E's decision. He said the utility companies could be fined up to $100,000 per day per incident for not following guidelines. Newsom responded in a statement to the media, saying, "The product of this investigation must be new rules and regulations. I also want to see customers not charged for PSPS. It seems obvious, but under the current rules, utilities can do just that. It's unacceptable and must be remedied."[14]

Addressing the issue of climate change, Hill called on both countries to take action:

> *To reduce the escalating threats from climate change, the United States, the world's second-largest emitter, and Australia, the world's largest exporter of coal, should cut their carbon footprints. In doing so, the countries can play leadership roles to keep global temperatures from rising to unmanageable, dangerous levels.*[15]

On March 2, 2020, NSW, Australia, had no bushfires. It was the first time without an active fire in more than 240 days, according to NSW Rural Fire Service. The state had survived another fire season, one of its worst on record. Thirty people died, and more than 27 million acres (11 million ha) were scorched, a size approximately equivalent to that of Virginia.[16] With the knowledge gleaned from each fire, coupled with technologies such as Phoenix and FROST, Australia's scientists, firefighters, and authorities moved forward. They planned to do their best to predict, prevent, and fight future wildfires. In this process, Australia aimed to become a good example for other nations.

Technology such as drones and FROST can help manage fires. Greg Mullins, who once served as commissioner of NSW Fire and Rescue, is clear about the importance of climate change. He spoke about the shortsightedness of fighting wildfires without addressing climate change, saying, "It's a bit like going to a gas fire and putting out all the houses and burning cars around it but not turning off the gas. Well, it'll keep burning. All the houses, everything: doesn't matter how much water you put on them, they'll keep catching fire again."[17]

> "SPECIFICALLY FOR THE WESTERN STATES, WE KNOW THAT THE WILDFIRE ACTIVITY IN RECENT DECADES—AT LEAST HALF OF IT—IS ATTRIBUTABLE TO HUMAN-CAUSED CLIMATE CHANGE."[18]
>
> **—KRISTINA DAHL, SENIOR CLIMATE SCIENTIST AT THE UNION OF CONCERNED SCIENTISTS**

Wildfires are not going away. Preparation is important for surviving them. Even better would be to prevent massive, deadly wildfires in the first place. Individuals, communities, agencies, organizations, and governments at multiple levels have an opportunity to take action. Numerous factors affect wildfires, from small, individual actions to large, global effects. While the overall picture may seem overwhelming, the good news is that each person can make choices to help create a positive difference in the story of the world's wildfires.

ESSENTIAL FACTS

MAJOR EVENTS

- In 2003, a wildfire in Siberia's subarctic forests destroys 47 million acres (19 million ha), making it the largest known fire in world history.
- In 2015, the burning of peat in Southeast Asia causes large amounts of dangerous smoke, likely contributing to the deaths of more than 100,000 people.
- In 2017, California has its most expensive and most destructive wildfire season on record.
- In 2019 and 2020, Australia has one of its worst bushfire seasons on record.

KEY PLAYERS

- The US Forest Service is the federal agency responsible for maintaining and protecting forests and grasslands in the United States, including by managing wildfires.

- New South Wales Rural Fire Service battled some of Australia's worst wildfires on record in the 2019–20 bushfire season.
- Cal Fire is the state of California's fire department and has battled increasingly intense wildfires in the late 2010s and early 2020s.

IMPACT ON SOCIETY

Wildfires cause considerable damage to the landscape, wildlife, and buildings, and they are often deadly. In recent decades, wildfires have increased in number and severity. The reasons for this include climate change, prescribed burning to clear land for agriculture, building in fire-prone areas, and faulty electrical equipment. Researchers and firefighters in the hardest-hit countries are working on understanding wildfires, including their causes, effects, and how to best fight them. Numerous people in different fields of study and employment related to wildfires are expecting the wildfire situation to worsen, with wildfires continuing to grow in number and strength. This will make their work even more important.

QUOTE

"We cannot just accept devastating wildfires as the 'new normal.' California is the global leader in technology and innovation. We can develop game-changing solutions and get ahead of this problem."

—Michael Picker, president, California Public Utilities Commission

GLOSSARY

COMMISSION
A group that performs the duties of administration or rulemaking for an activity.

FIRE RETARDANT
A material used to prevent something from burning.

FOSSIL FUEL
A natural fuel, such as coal or gas, which contributes to global climate change.

INSULATION
A covering that helps keep a steady internal temperature.

LODGEPOLE
A type of tree that releases its seeds as a result of wildfire heat.

METEOROLOGIST
A scientist who studies weather patterns.

MITIGATE
To make something less intense.

NONCOMBUSTIBLE
Not flammable; fire-resistant.

PEAT
Soil formed from partially decomposed plant matter, typically found in cold, boggy, acidic ground.

RESIN
A thick, sticky substance produced by certain plants or trees.

SAVANNA
A treeless plain.

SMOLDER
To burn slowly and without a flame.

WILDLAND
Land that has not been developed by humans.

ADDITIONAL RESOURCES

SELECTED BIBLIOGRAPHY

"A Visual Guide to the Bushfire Crisis." *BBC News*, 31 Jan. 2020, bbc.com. Accessed 30 Apr. 2020.

Pierre-Louis, Kendra. "The Amazon, Siberia, Indonesia: A World of Fire." *New York Times*, 4 Sept. 2019, nytimes.com. Accessed 30 Apr. 2020.

Schmidt, Amanda. "How Destructive Wildfires Create Their Own Weather." *AccuWeather*, 2020, accuweather.com. Accessed 30 Apr. 2020.

FURTHER READINGS

Ferguson, Gary. *Land on Fire*. Timber Press, 2017.

Peters, Scott, and S. D. Brown. *I Escaped the California Camp Fires*. Toppsta, 2019.

Williams-Noren, Carolyn. *Catastrophes in the Twenty-First Century*. ReferencePoint Press, 2020.

ONLINE RESOURCES

To learn more about the world's wildfires, please visit **abdobooklinks.com** or scan this QR code. These links are routinely monitored and updated to provide the most current information available.

MORE INFORMATION

For more information on this subject, contact or visit the following organizations:

California Department of Forestry and Fire Protection (Cal Fire)
1416 Ninth St.
Sacramento, CA 94244
916-653-5123
fire.ca.gov
Cal Fire is the state of California's fire department, tasked with preventing wildfires and keeping the state's forests safe.

Missoula Fire Sciences Laboratory
5775 US Highway 10 W.
Missoula, MT 59808-9361
406-329-4800
firelab.org
The Missoula Fire Sciences Lab, part of the US Forest Service, researches many aspects of wildfires. Through its research, the lab advises lawmakers on how to prevent future fires.

SOURCE NOTES

CHAPTER 1. AUSTRALIA BURNING

1. Jessie Yeung, Isaac Yee, and Sheena McKenzie. "Thousands of Australian Residents Had to Take Refuge on a Beach as Wildfires Raged." *CNN*, 31 Dec. 2019, cnn.com. Accessed 31 Aug. 2020.
2. Bill Chappell. "Officials in Australia's New South Wales Celebrate: 'All Fires Are Now Contained.'" *NPR*, 13 Feb. 2020, npr.org. Accessed 31 Aug. 2020.
3. "Australian Bushfires: A Timeline of What's Happened So Far." *Create*, 20 Jan. 2020, createdigital.org.au. Accessed 31 Aug. 2020.
4. "Australian Bushfires."
5. "Australian Bushfires."
6. "Australian Bushfires."
7. "Bushfire Weather." *Australian Bureau of Meteorology*, 2020, bom.gov.au. Accessed 31 Aug. 2020.
8. "Australian Bushfires."
9. "Australian Bushfires."
10. Peter Bodo and Simon Cambers. "Australian Open FAQ: How Bushfires Could Impact Tennis' First Grand Slam of 2020." *ESPN*, 20 Jan. 2020, espn.com. Accessed 31 Aug. 2020.
11. Eleanor Ainge Roy and Kate Lyons. "New Zealand Sends Troops to Help with Australian Bushfires as Pacific Nations Offer Support." *Guardian*, 5 Jan. 2020, theguardian.com. Accessed 31 Aug. 2020.
12. Bodo and Cambers, "Australian Open FAQ."
13. "A Visual Guide to the Bushfire Crisis." *BBC*, 31 Jan. 2020, bbc.com. Accessed 31 Aug. 2020.
14. Ella Torres. "Fires in New South Wales Contained for the First Time Since Australia's Fire Season Began." *ABC News*, 13 Feb. 2020, abcnews.go.com. Accessed 31 Aug. 2020.
15. Marc Lallanilla. "Australia's Wildfires: Are Eucalyptus Trees to Blame?" *Live Science*, 21 Oct. 2013, livescience.com. Accessed 31 Aug. 2020.
16. Damien Cave. "The End of Australia as We Know It." *New York Times*, 15 Feb. 2020, nytimes.com. Accessed 31 Aug. 2020.
17. Mihir Zaveri and Emily S. Rueb. "How Many Animals Have Died in Australia's Wildfires?" *New York Times*, 11 Jan. 2020, nytimes.com. Accessed 31 Aug. 2020.
18. Zaveri and Rueb, "How Many Animals?"
19. Zaveri and Rueb, "How Many Animals?"

CHAPTER 2. WILDFIRE BASICS

1. Claire Asher. "Why We Should Let Raging Wildfires Burn." *BBC*, 25 July 2016, bbc.com. Accessed 31 Aug. 2020.
2. Kevin Bonsor. "How Wildfires Work." *HowStuffWorks*, 2020, howstuffworks.com. Accessed 31 Aug. 2020.
3. "Elements of Fire." *Smokey Bear*, 2020, smokeybear.com. Accessed 31 Aug. 2020.
4. "U.S. Wildfire Risk Worsening, According to Climate Projections." *Science Daily*, 4 Dec. 2012, sciencedaily.com. Accessed 31 Aug. 2020.

CHAPTER 3. A HISTORY OF WILDFIRES

1. Kim Estep. "The Peshtigo Fire." *National Weather Service*, n.d., weather.gov. Accessed 31 Aug. 2020.
2. Everett Rosenfeld. "The Peshtigo Fire, 1871." *Time*, 8 June 2011, time.com. Accessed 31 Aug. 2020.
3. Estep, "The Peshtigo Fire."
4. Rosenfeld, "The Peshtigo Fire, 1871."
5. "Moose Lake and Cloquet Fires of October 1918." *National Weather Service*, n.d., weather.gov. Accessed 31 Aug. 2020.
6. Stephen T. Schroth. "Cloquet, Minnesota, Fire (1918)." *SAGE Reference*, 2020, sk.sagepub.com. Accessed 31 Aug. 2020.
7. Iemima Ploscariu. "Largest Brush and Forest Fires in Recorded History." *World Atlas*, 15 Mar. 2018, worldatlas.com. Accessed 31 Aug. 2020.
8. "Black Friday 1939." *Forest Fire Management Victoria*, 6 Oct. 2017, ffm.vic.gov.au. Accessed 31 Aug. 2020.
9. "Black Friday Bushfires, 1939." *Australian Institute for Disaster Resilience*, n.d., aidr.org.au. Accessed 31 Aug. 2020.
10. Jenny Wilson. "Daxing'anling Wildfire, China, 1987." *Time*, 8 June 2011, time.com. Accessed 31 Aug. 2020.
11. Wilson, "Daxing'anling Wildfire, China, 1987."
12. K.G. Hirsch. "Canadian Forest Service Publications." *Canada*, 1991, nrcan.gc.ca. Accessed 31 Aug. 2020.
13. Nate Rawlings. "Indonesia Wildfire, 1997." *Time*, 8 June 2011, time.com. Accessed 31 Aug. 2020.
14. Ploscariu, "Largest Brush and Forest Fires."
15. Nick Carbone. "The Cedar Fire, Southern California, 2003." *Time*, 8 June 2011, time.com. Accessed 31 Aug. 2020.
16. "Cedar Fire." *CBS News*, 13 Sept. 2007, cbsnews.com. *Wayback Machine*, web.archive.org. Accessed 31 Aug. 2020.
17. Everett Rosenfeld. "Greece, 2007." *Time*, 8 June 2011, time.com. Accessed 31 Aug. 2020.
18. "Black Saturday Bushfires." *National Museum Australia*, 17 June 2020, nma.gov.au. Accessed 31 Aug. 2020.
19. Chloe Hooper. "On the Arsonist's Trail: Inside Australia's Worst Bushfire Catastrophe." *Guardian*, 24 May 2019, theguardian.com. Accessed 31 Aug. 2020.
20. "America's Most Devastating Wildfires." *PBS*, 2020, pbs.org. Accessed 31 Aug. 2020.
21. Brian Kahn. "Fires in NW Territories in Line with 'Unprecedented' Burn." *Climate Central*, 17 July 2014, climatecentral.org. Accessed 31 Aug. 2020.

CHAPTER 4. MORE FIRES, BIGGER FIRES

1. "Unexpected Ways Animals Influence Fires." *Science Daily*, 5 Mar. 2020, sciencedaily.com. Accessed 31 Aug. 2020.
2. Kasha Patel. "Six Trends to Know about Fire Season in the Western U.S." *NASA*, 5 Dec. 2018, nasa.gov. Accessed 31 Aug. 2020.
3. Patel, "Six Trends to Know."
4. Patel, "Six Trends to Know."
5. Amanda Schmidt. "How Destructive Wildfires Create Their Own Weather." *AccuWeather*, 2020, accuweather.com. Accessed 31 Aug. 2020.
6. Tim Schauenberg. "Wildfires: Climate Change and Deforestation Increase the Global Risk." *DW*, 8 Jan. 2020, dw.com. Accessed 31 Aug. 2020.
7. Schauenberg, "Wildfires."
8. "Area Burned in 2019 Forest Fires in Indonesia Exceeds 2018." *Reuters*, 21 Oct. 2019, reuters.com. Accessed 31 Aug. 2020.
9. "Replanting After California Wildfires." *National Forest Foundation*, n.d., nationalforests.org. Accessed 31 Aug. 2020.
10. Kendra Pierre-Louis. "The Amazon, Siberia, Indonesia: A World of Fire." *New York Times*, 4 Sept. 2019, nytimes.com. Accessed 31 Aug. 2020.

CHAPTER 5. WHY ARE FIRES GETTING WORSE?

1. "Weather, Global Warming and Climate Change." *NASA*, n.d., nasa.gov. Accessed 31 Aug. 2020.
2. Robinson Meyer. "Why the Wildfires of 2018 Have Been So Ferocious." *Atlantic*, 10 Aug. 2018, theatlantic.com. Accessed 31 Aug. 2020.

SOURCE NOTES CONTINUED

3. "Wildfires Have Gotten Bigger in Recent Years, and the Trend Is Likely to Continue." *Washington Post*, 14 Aug. 2018, washingtonpost.com. Accessed 31 Aug. 2020.

4. Meyer, "Why the Wildfires."

5. Thomas Fuller and Julie Turkewitz. "'The New Normal': Wildfires Roar Across the West, Again." *New York Times*, 2 July 2018, nytimes.com. Accessed 31 Aug. 2020.

6. Meyer, "Why the Wildfires."

7. Kasha Patel. "Six Trends to Know about Fire Season in the Western U.S." *NASA*, 5 Dec. 2018, nasa.gov. Accessed 31 Aug. 2020.

8. Lindsay Schnell. "Battling Wildfires Year-Round Is Now the Norm. How Did We Get Here?" *USA Today*, 15 Nov. 2018, usatoday.com. Accessed 31 Aug. 2020.

9. Mia Rabson. "Climate Change Driving Up Risk of Wildfires in Canada: Fire Experts." *Global News*, 8 Jan. 2020, globalnews.ca. Accessed 31 Aug. 2020.

10. Rabson, "Climate Change."

11. Rabson, "Climate Change."

12. Scott H. Black et al. "Do Bark Beetle Outbreaks Increase Wildfire Risks in the Central U.S. Rocky Mountains? Implications from Recent Research." *BioOne*, 1 Jan. 2013, bioone.org. Accessed 31 Aug. 2020.

13. Rabson, "Climate Change."

14. Rabson, "Climate Change."

15. Jake Rudnitsky et al. "The World's Largest Forest Has Been on Fire for Months." *Bloomberg*, 8 Aug. 2019, bloomberg.com. Accessed 31 Aug. 2020.

16. Tim Schauenberg. "Wildfires: Climate Change and Deforestation Increase the Global Risk." *DW*, 8 Jan. 2020, dw.com. Accessed 31 Aug. 2020.

17. Kendra Pierre-Louis. "The Amazon, Siberia, Indonesia: A World of Fire." *New York Times*, 4 Sept. 2019, nytimes.com. Accessed 31 Aug. 2020.

18. Schauenberg, "Wildfires."

19. Pierre-Louis, "The Amazon, Siberia, Indonesia."

20. Kendra Pierre-Louis and Jeremy White. "Americans Are Moving Closer to Nature, and to Fire Danger." *New York Times*, 15 Nov. 2018, nytimes.com. Accessed 31 Aug. 2020.

21. Julie Cart and Judy Lin. "California Fires Are Getting Worse. What's Going On?" *LAist*, 28 Oct. 2019, laist.com. Accessed 31 Aug. 2020.

22. Fuller and Turkewitz, "'The New Normal.'"

23. Cart and Lin, "California Fires."

24. Cart and Lin, "California Fires."

25. Priyanka Boghani. "Camp Fire: By the Numbers." *PBS*, 29 Oct. 2019, pbs.org. Accessed 31 Aug. 2020.

26. Doug Stanglin et al. "'This Is Very Sad to See': Trump Surveys California Wildfire Devastation After 76 Killed." *USA Today*, 17 Nov. 2018, usatoday.com. Accessed 31 Aug. 2020.

CHAPTER 6. THE COSTS OF WILDFIRES

1. Julie Cart and Judy Lin. "California Fires Are Getting Worse. What's Going On?" *LAist*, 28 Oct. 2019, laist.com. Accessed 31 Aug. 2020.
2. Cart and Lin, "California Fires."
3. Kimberly Amadeo. "How Wildfires Impact the Economy." *Balance*, 28 Aug. 2020, thebalance.com. Accessed 31 Aug. 2020.
4. Gabrielle Levy. "Wildfires Are Getting Worse, And More Costly, Every Year." *U.S. News*, 1 Aug. 2018, usnews.com. Accessed 31 Aug. 2020.
5. Amadeo, "How Wildfires Impact the Economy."
6. Joe Cochrane. "Blazes in Southeast Asia May Have Led to Deaths of Over 100,000, Study Says." *New York Times*, 19 Sept. 2016, nytimes.com. Accessed 31 Aug. 2020.
7. Paul Reed and Richard Denniss. "With Costs Approaching $100 Billion, the Fires Are Australia's Costliest Natural Disaster." *Conversation*, 16 Jan. 2020, theconversation.com. Accessed 31 Aug. 2020.
8. Kendra Pierre-Louis. "The Amazon, Siberia, Indonesia: A World of Fire." *New York Times*, 4 Sept. 2019, nytimes.com. Accessed 31 Aug. 2020.
9. "Pentagon Says Climate Change-Driven Wildfires Are Growing National Security Threat." *CPR*, 13 Feb. 2020, cpr.org. Accessed 31 Aug. 2020.
10. Brian Resnick et al. "8 Things Everyone Should Know about Australia's Wildfire Disaster." *Vox*, 22 Jan. 2020, vox.com. Accessed 31 Aug. 2020.
11. Cart and Lin, "California Fires."

CHAPTER 7. FIGHTING WILDFIRES

1. Mira Rojanasakul and Hayley Warren. "What a Hotter and Drier World Means for Shared Firefighting." *Bloomberg Green*, 9 Apr. 2020, bloomberg.com. Accessed 31 Aug. 2020.
2. "Wildfire Technology Innovation Summit." *FireTech Summit*, n.d., firetechsummit.cpus.ca.gov. Accessed 31 Aug. 2020.
3. Rojanasakul and Warren, "What a Hotter and Drier World Means."

CHAPTER 8. PREVENTION

1. Kendra Pierre-Louis and Jeremy White. "Americans Are Moving Closer to Nature, and to Fire Danger." *New York Times*, 15 Nov. 2018, nytimes.com. Accessed 31 Aug. 2020.
2. Susie Cagle. "'Fire Is Medicine': The Tribes Burning California Forests to Save Them." *Guardian*, 21 Nov. 2019, theguardian.com. Accessed 31 Aug. 2020.
3. "Prescribed Fires." *Smokey Bear*, 2020, smokeybear.com. Accessed 31 Aug. 2020.
4. Lindsay Schnell. "Battling Wildfires Year-Round Is Now the Norm. How Did We Get Here?" *USA Today*, 15 Nov. 2018, usatoday.com. Accessed 31 Aug. 2020.
5. Don Thompson. "California Adopts 22 New Laws Taking Aim at Wildfire Danger." *KPBS*, 2 Oct. 2019, kpbs.org. Accessed 31 Aug. 2020.
6. Schnell, "Battling Wildfires."
7. "Controlled Burn Morphs into Wildfire in Alabama." *AP*, 17 Apr. 2020, apnews.com. Accessed 31 Aug. 2020.
8. "Why We Work with Fire." *Nature Conservancy*, 28 June 2019, nature.org. Accessed 31 Aug. 2020.
9. Schnell, "Battling Wildfires."
10. Schnell, "Battling Wildfires."
11. Oliver Milman. "Huge Rise of People at Risk from Wildfires as Western US Population Grows." *Guardian*, 8 Aug. 2018, theguardian.com. Accessed 31 Aug. 2020.
12. Milman, "Huge Rise of People."
13. Gavin Newsom. "California Opens Investigation into Utility Companies Shutting Off Power." *CBS Sacramento*, 29 Oct. 2019, sacramento.cbslocal.com. Accessed 31 Aug. 2020.
14. Newsom, "California Opens Investigation."
15. Alice C. Hill. "Australia's Fires Will Rage Again. Here's How the Government Can Prepare." *Council on Foreign Relations*, 9 Jan. 2020, cfr.org. Accessed 31 Aug. 2020.
16. Vanessa Romo. "All Bushfires Extinguished in Australia's Hardest-Hit New South Wales, Officials Say." *NPR*, 2 Mar. 2020, npr.org. Accessed 31 Aug. 2020.
17. Helen Sullivan. "Australia's Fire Season Ends, and Researchers Look to the Next One." *New York Times*, 21 Apr. 2020, nytimes.com. Accessed 31 Aug. 2020.
18. "The Wildfire Debate: What's the Cause of these Massive NorCal Fires?" *Active NorCal*, 9 Sept. 2018, activenorcal.com. Accessed 31 Aug. 2020.

INDEX

ABOUT THE AUTHOR

REBECCA ROWELL

Rebecca Rowell has put her degree in publishing and writing to work as an editor and as an author, working on dozens of books. Recent topics as an author include the Paris climate agreement and the history of criminal law in the United States. She lives in Minneapolis, Minnesota.

ABOUT THE CONSULTANT

CRYSTAL RAYMOND, PhD

Crystal Raymond has a PhD in forest ecology and has studied wildfire and climate resilience for more than 15 years. She works on translating science into actionable information to help the public plan and prepare for the impacts of climate change, especially more frequent wildfires. She lives in Seattle, Washington, where she enjoys hiking and camping with her husband and two children.